AGING WEL

THE AGING FAMILY AND MARRIAGE

PETER MENCONI

MT. SAGE PUBLISHING

Mt. Sage Publishing
Centennial, CO 80122

Scriptures taken from the Holy Bible, New International Version®, NIV®. Copyright © 1973, 1978, 1984, 2011 by Biblica, Inc.™ Used by permission of Zondervan. All rights reserved worldwide. www.zondervan.com The "NIV" and "New International Version" are trademarks registered in the United States Patent and Trademark Office by Biblica, Inc.™

TABLE OF CONTENTS

SESSION 1: The New Family   11

SESSION 2: Family Conflict   19

SESSION 3: Sandwich Generation   27

SESSION 4: Adult Children   35

SESSION 5: Empty Nest   43

SESSION 6: The Aging Marriage   51

ABOUT THE CASA NETWORK

In 1983, three Southern California churches established the CASA Network ministry to serve their 50+ members through cooperative efforts. The first jointly sponsored one day event was called Jamboree (now Life Celebration). The response to this first event led to a three day retreat held at a Christian conference center. A committee representing various churches met the next year to discover how to meet the growing needs of the Christian adult senior community and to discuss incorporating. They determined that the name of the new organization would be called CASA, Christian Association of Senior Adults.

In 1993 the CASA Board of Directors caught the vision to broaden its ministry to mid and post career age men and women nationally and internationally. In the fall of 1994, CASA launched two quarterly publications – The Energizer for senior adults and Energizing Leaders for leaders of Adults 50+ in the local church. With the explosion of the Boomer generation, a third quarterly publication was launched in 2001 for this population, called Legacy Living. For a time, CASA engaged in a website partnership with Christianity Today.

From 1993 through 1998 regional leadership training conferences were offered to pastors and lay leaders of adult 50+ ministries in a number of states and Canada. In 1998, the first National Leadership Training Conference was held in Irvine, CA and brought together over 300 pastors and lay leaders from 26 states and Canada. A further development in the growth of CASA's ministry was the establishment of a website **www.gocasa.org** that provides resources and information on 50+ ministry. Serving leaders across the country, the CASA Network offers regional, national, and international 50+ leadership conferences. You can access the CASA Network website at **www.gocasa.org** for the latest information on training offerings.

Today, the CASA Network is a premier training and equipping source for the Church's ministry to midlife and beyond age men and women. Augmented by internet and print media, the CASA Network brings together an array of leaders within the field of 50+ ministry to inspire and equip the Church for ministry to and through adults in life's second half. Only God knows how many lives have been touched, how many churches have been changed, how many leaders have been trained because of the vision and leadership of the CASA Network. Check us out at **www.gocasa.org** and welcome to the CASA Network Aging Well Bible Study Series.

BEFORE YOU BEGIN!
Instructions on how to get the most out of this book.

The primary purpose of this Bible study is to help you to take a closer look at your aging marriage and/or family and see how you can maximize these relationships.

This book contains six Bible study sessions on the topics of contemporary families and marriages that can be done individually or in a small group. The studies are written for people who have never studied the Bible, occasionally study the Bible, or often study the Bible. That is, virtually everyone interested in aging marriages and families will benefit from these studies. Each session allows the Bible to speak to where you are and where God may want you to go.

While these studies can be done individually, they are primarily designed to be done in a small group setting. In fact, you will receive maximum benefit when the study is discussed in a group. The more diverse your group is in age and experience, the more you will learn from these studies.

SUGGESTIONS ON FORMING A GROUP

1. Form a group that has between eight and 15 members. Groups larger or smaller are generally less effective.

2. One person should be appointed as the group facilitator. The facilitator's primary role is to get everyone together at an appointed time and place. The facilitator also gets the study started and keeps it going without getting off track. After the initial meeting the facilitator role can rotate within the group.

3. At the first meeting have the group members introduce themselves to one another and have each person share his or her responses to the following questions:

a) Where were you born and raised?

b) Where were you and what were you doing at age 10? Age 18? Age 25?

c) What one person, place, or experience has had the greatest impact on your life and why?

4. Before starting the study group members should agree on the length and frequency of meeting times. Normally, each study should take about one hour. All group members should commit themselves to attending all group sessions, unless there are circumstances beyond their control.

5. Give time for the small group to gel. Don't expect everything to click in the first session or two.

Because the interaction in a small group can reach into personal areas, it is important that group members agree upon "ground rules."

SUGGESTED GROUND RULES FOR SMALL GROUP STUDY

1. Jesus said that "the Holy Spirit, whom the Father will send in my name, will teach you all things and will remind you of everything I said to you." With this in mind, each group session should open in prayer asking the Holy Spirit to teach and guide. (Not everyone needs to pray. If a person is uncomfortable praying in public, he or she should be given freedom to remain silent.)

2. No one or two persons should dominate the discussion time. All group members should have an equal opportunity to express their thoughts, feelings, and experiences.

3. Because people's experiences and perspectives vary, there will be ideas, thoughts, and feelings expressed which will be quite diverse. All members should respect one another's perspective.

4. Confidentiality on what is said in the study should be agreed upon by all group members.

5. If significant conflict arises between specific group members, they should make every effort to resolve this conflict apart from group time. That is, they should agree to meet together at another time to discuss their differences.

6. If the group ends in prayer, members should pray for one another.

SESSION 1 | THE NEW FAMILY

INTRODUCTION
Have one or more group members read the introduction aloud.

The Issue: Families have changed from what they were 50 years ago. What is your attitude toward the ways families have changed?

Remember the days when father knew best? Those days are long gone. Ward, June, Wally and Beaver Cleaver no longer live next door. Ozzie, Harriett, David and Ricky Nelson are not living down the street. Even the Brady bunch is no longer in the neighborhood.

In the past 50 years the American family has profoundly changed... and there are numerous reasons why. A dramatic rise in the divorce rate from the 1960s has disrupted family stability. (The U.S. has the highest divorce rate among developed nations.) More couples are cohabitating or living together before marriage than ever before. In 1960, there were about 450,000 cohabitating couples. Today, there are more than 7 million unmarried couples living together. The legalization of gay marriages has also altered the family landscape.

Today, young people are waiting longer to marry. For women, the average age for a first time marriage is 27; for men, it is 29. For most 20-somethings, marriage and family can wait as they explore the many options available to them. In addition, the traditional order of marriage and then having children has been flipped on its head. Today, about half of all first born children are born to unmarried women. And unfortunately, research shows that children with an absent or semi-permanent father face a tougher time than children in two-parent families.

The single parent family phenomenon has altered the lives of many older adults who thought their childrearing days were over. Today, millions of grandparents have full or part-time child care responsibilities for their grandchildren. In fact, over 5 million children live in grandparent headed households. Without the loving interventions and sacrifices of grandparents, the current instability of American families would be even greater than it is. Many researchers view family instability as one of the greatest risks to the well being of children.

The phenomenon of the stepfamily is another change that has altered the look of our family units. It is estimated that these blended families are the predominant family form in the United States. And the blending of a stepfamily is usually quite complex for a multiple of reasons. The starting of a new marriage, the blending of different histories and personalities, the clash of different philosophies of childrearing, and new sibling rivalry are just a few of the challenges.

In addition to these changes in the American family, we are seeing families becoming more diverse. According to the 2010 census, the multiracial population among children increased by about 50 per cent from the year 2000. Today, many families look significantly different than they did 50 years ago. In many cases, older adults have had to adjust to having multiracial grandchildren. For followers of Jesus Christ the changes in families today afford new opportunities to grow and show the love of God.

YOUR TAKE

From the following list, check the responses that best describe how you think and feel about the ways families have changed.

___ I think families have changed for the worse.

___ I think families have changed for the better.

___ Families are more complex than they used to be.

___ Families are pretty much the same, because family members still love one another.

___ Families are in big trouble today.

___ Families can use a lot of help.

___ Families are still the backbone of our nation.

___ Other _____.

Why did you answer as you did?

YOUR REFLECTION

Read the following passages from the Bible and answer the questions that follow.

Coming to his hometown, he began teaching the people in their synagogue, and they were amazed. "Where did this man get this wisdom and these miraculous powers?" they asked. "Isn't this the carpenter's son? Isn't his mother's name Mary, and aren't his brothers James, Joseph, Simon and Judas? Aren't all his sisters with us? Where then did this man get all these things?"
—*Matthew 13:54-56*

1. Jesus was a member of a human family. What do you think it would be like to have Jesus Christ as your child or sibling?

2. Do you think their neighbors noticed anything different about Joseph, Mary, and their children? Why? Why not?

While Jesus was still talking to the crowd, his mother and brothers stood outside, wanting to speak to him. Someone told him, "Your mother and brothers are standing outside, wanting to speak to you."

*He replied to him, "Who is my mother, and who are my brothers?"
Pointing to his disciples, he said, "Here are my mother and my brothers. For whoever does the will of my Father in heaven is my brother
and sister and mother."*
—Matthew 12:46-50

3. From these verses, what insights do you get about Jesus' relationship with his mother and brothers?

4. What was Jesus teaching the crowd in his response regarding his
family?

5. Do you think Jesus was being disrespectful to his mother and
brothers? Please explain your response.

6. If you were Jesus and knew that your family wanted to speak to you,
how would you have responded? How would you have responded?

YOUR APPLICATION

During the coming week think about the following questions.

1. Spend some time this week thinking about the ways your family has changed in the past 10 to 20 years. Have these changes been positive or negative?

2. Spend some time this week reflecting on your extended family and families of your friends. In want ways do these families represent the ways families have changed in the past decade or two?

3. Spend some time looking at families in the Bible. Were these families trouble free? How did God relate to these families? (Suggested families to read about: Adam and Eve's family; Noah's family; Abraham's family; King David's family)

SESSION 2 | FAMILY CONFLICT

INTRODUCTION
Have one or more group members read the introduction aloud.

The Issue: Virtually every family experiences some conflict. What are the sources of conflict in your family and how can you best respond to this family conflict?

Family conflict is quite common. Since most families are made up of several generations, family members often have different views, beliefs, and behaviors that clash. If occasional conflict is talked through and resolved, family relationships can deepen. But when conflict between family members is not handled well, arguments, stress, alienation, and estrangement can result.

There can be numerous reasons for family conflict. Changes in a family, like separation and divorce, can cause conflict. Even remarriage, a happy occasion, can cause tension and stress as a new couple and family learn to live together. The birth of a child or grandchild can cause family conflict. Raising teenagers is often a time of stress and tension for both parents and children. Financial and job stresses are a common source of family conflict. Still yet, political and religious views can cause family members to drift apart.

Older adults in families can experience some unique family conflict. Adult children who have returned home and "failed to launch" can make life more difficult. Health issues that require care giving and care receiving can strain family relationships, especially if they involve major medical expenses. Retirement can create conflict between a couple that is not used to spending so much time together. And retirees can experience a difficult time adjusting to a life without a schedule or work purpose.

But without question, the greatest source of family conflict and tension has been caused by divorce. While almost no one enters marriage expecting to fail, the divorce rate in America for first marriages is between 41% and 50%. The rate of marriage breakups for second marriages is from 60% to 67% and the rate for third marriages is about 75%.

Divorce brings a whole new set of conflicts to a family. If precipitated by unfaithfulness, issues of anger and unforgiveness often persist. Battles over finances and the custody of children or grandchildren can further inflame family relationships. When children or grandchildren are involved, the juggling of schedules can create major stress and conflict. Today, many grandparents have stepped in to cushion grandchildren from some of the negative impacts of their parents' divorce. But grandparent intervention can create new conflicts.

Adding to the mix of family instability is the increase in the number of family members who stay single or choose to cohabitate. In America, over 50% of couples are living together without being married. Of these couples, about 50% of cohabitating couples get married for the first time. When adult children cohabitate, it often creates tension and conflict with their parents who were raised in a different era with different views of marriage and cohabitation,

Whatever the causes of family conflict, older adults have an opportunity to be part of the solutions and not a contributor to the problems. Older adults can bring wisdom to family relationships that are centered in love. This is especially true for followers of Christ. Jesus has called us to love one another and nowhere is love needed more than in our families. God is love and the source of all love. Whether you are single, the parent of little or big children, or a grandparent, you have an opportunity to influence your family and others through love. Look around. What the world needs now is love.

YOUR TAKE

From the following list, check the responses that best answers the questions. Discuss your responses with your group.

1. What do you see as the greatest causes of family conflict?

__ Finances	__ Parenting philosophy
__ Work and career	__ Sibling rivalry
__ Children/teenagers	__ Divorce issues
__ In-laws	__ Spiritual views
__ Sexual relationships	__ Political views
__ Lack of respect	__ Poor communication
__ Anger	__ Unrealistic expectations
__ Lack of trust	__ Physical abuse
__ Housework	__ Other _____

2. In the past, how have you successfully or unsuccessfully addressed family conflict?

YOUR REFLECTION

Read the following passages from the Bible and answer the questions that follow.

Joseph had a dream, and when he told it to his brothers, they hated him all the more. He said to them, "Listen to this dream I had: We were binding sheaves of grain out in the field when suddenly my sheaf rose and stood upright, while your sheaves gathered around mine and bowed down to it."

His brothers said to him, "Do you intend to reign over us? Will you actually rule us?" And they hated him all the more because of his dream and what he had said.

Then he had another dream, and he told it to his brothers. "Listen," he said, "I had another dream, and this time the sun and moon and eleven stars were bowing down to me."

When he told his father as well as his brothers, his father rebuked him and said, "What is this dream you had? Will your mother and I and your brothers actually come and bow down to the ground before you?" His brothers were jealous of him, but his father kept the matter in mind.
—Genesis 37: 5-11

The story continues with Joseph's brothers plotting to kill him. Instead, they sell him into slavery.

Judah said to his brothers, "What will we gain if we kill our brother and cover up his blood? Come, let's sell him to the Ishmaelites and not lay our hands on him; after all, he is our brother, our own flesh and blood." His brothers agreed.

So when the Midianite merchants came by, his brothers pulled Joseph up out of the cistern and sold him for twenty shekels of silver to the Ishmaelites, who took him to Egypt.
—Genesis 37: 26-28

1. Why did Joseph's brothers hate him? Did you experience sibling rivalry growing up? If so, how has it affected you?

2. In what ways did "blood being thicker than water" affect the outcome of Joseph's life? Have you had a similar experience with a family member that changed the way you reacted? If so, please share that experience.

3. In what ways did God use conflict in Jacob's family to fulfill his purposes?

Every year Jesus' parents went to Jerusalem for the Festival of the Passover. When he was twelve years old, they went up to the festival, according to the custom. After the festival was over, while his parents were returning home, the boy Jesus stayed behind in Jerusalem, but they were unaware of it. Thinking he was in their company, they traveled on for a day. Then they began looking for him among their relatives and friends. When they did not find him, they went back to Jerusalem to look for him. After three days they found him in the temple courts, sitting among the teachers, listening to them and asking them questions. Everyone who heard him was amazed at his understanding and his answers. When his parents saw him, they were astonished. His mother said to him, "Son, why have you treated us like this? Your father and I have been anxiously searching for you."

"Why were you searching for me?" he asked. "Didn't you know I had to be in my Father's house?" But they did not understand what he was saying to them.

Then he went down to Nazareth with them and was obedient to them. But his mother treasured all these things in her heart. And Jesus grew in wisdom and stature, and in favor with God and man.
—Luke 2: 41-52

4. From this account, do you think Mary and Joseph were negligent parents?

5. From these verses, what can we infer about the role of the extended family in the lives of the nuclear family? That is, did relatives and friends play a more important role than they do today?

6. Was there conflict between Jesus and his parents? If so, what was the source of that conflict?

YOUR APPLICATION

During the coming week think about the following questions.

1. Spend some time thinking about your family: your family of origin; your current family; your extended family; your spiritual family; etc. How would you assess the health of your family relationships?

2. Are you currently experiencing family conflict? If so, how might you be a peacemaker in this conflict? Spend some time this week asking God to give you the wisdom to reduce this conflict.

SESSION 3 | SANDWICH GENERATION

▌INTRODUCTION
Have one or more group members read the introduction aloud.

The Issue: More and more people are joining the sandwich generation as they care for aging parents, adult children, and grandchildren. How can the Christian community best minister to the caregivers in the sandwich generation?

Today more and more older adults are providing physical, financial, and emotional support for their parents, spouses, adult children and grandchildren. In fact, recent surveys show that about one-in-seven middle aged adults are providing support for both an aging parent and a child. As people live longer and young people have more difficulty becoming financially independent, more and more middle-aged and older adults find themselves caring for two or three generations. These are the members of the "sandwich generation."

Several demographic trends have come together to create the sandwich generation. As life expectancy has increased, it is not unusual to have members of two generations in the same family that are older than 65 years of age. Aging adults can find themselves helping to care and support their parents while trying to save and plan for their own retirement. The time and money needed to care for aging parents may result in the need for older adults to work longer than desired. Add to these responsibilities the potential need for older adults to help support adult children who are having difficulty establishing financial and emotional stability.

Another trend that has added pressure and complications to the lives of some members of the sandwich generation is the need to raise their grandchildren. It is estimated that about 3 million grandparents have responsibility for about 8 million grandchildren. There are numerous reasons why these "grandfamilies" come together: a parent's death, drug addiction and abuse, military deployment, incarceration, mental illness, and more.

Needless to say, members of the sandwich generation can use help. While sympathetic employers can help, churches have opportunities to get creative in providing assistance. Unfortunately, churches have been slow to respond to the needs of older adults and their families. Increasingly, as congregations continue to age, churches will feel more and more pressure to respond to these needs. Churches can provide a network of support and encouragement to caregivers by providing periodic relief through volunteers. In addition, churches can offer seminars and workshops to proactively prepare older adults of the sandwich generation.

Caregiving is central to the lives of the sandwich generation. And among all the people in our society, followers of Jesus Christ are called to care for others. Caregiving, whether physical, financial, emotional or spiritual, is a stressful experience. Compassionate church congregations have many opportunities to lovingly come along side caregivers to "hold up their arms" as they serve others.

YOUR TAKE

From the following list, check the responses that best answers the questions. Discuss your responses with your group.

1. Which of the following statements best expresses your view of your responsibility to the other generations in your family?

___ Adult children have the responsibility of caring for their aging parents.

___ Parents have a responsibility to provide financial support for their struggling adult children.

___ Parents should let their adult children "figure out" life, even when they struggle.

___ Adult children should expect their aging parents to take care of themselves.

___ Every member of the family should be responsible for themselves.

__ Grandparents should play no role in supporting their grandchildren.

__ Parents who indulge their adult children are doing them a disservice.

__ Family members should pull together to help each other in any way possible.

__ Other _____.

2. What is your attitude toward caregiving and caregivers?

__ Caregiving allows your loved ones to live as independently as possible.

__ Caregivers need to take care of themselves.

__ Caregivers need to learn strategies for planning and problem-solving.

__ Caregiving should involve friends, neighbors, and other relatives whenever possible.

__ Caregiving to aging parents should only be done by professionals.

__ Caregivers should determine what they can and cannot do.

__ Caregivers should take seminars and workshops on caregiving.

__ Caregivers should take advantage of community resources.

YOUR REFLECTION

Read the following passages from the Bible and answer the questions that follow.

Do not rebuke an older man harshly, but exhort him as if he were your father. Treat younger men as brothers, older women as mothers, and younger women as sisters, with absolute purity.

Give proper recognition to those widows who are really in need. But if a widow has children or grandchildren, these should learn first of all to put their religion into practice by caring for their own family and so repaying their parents and grandparents, for this is pleasing to God. The widow who is really in need and left all alone puts her hope in God and continues night and day to pray and to ask God for help. But the widow who lives for pleasure is dead even while she lives. Give the people these instructions, so that no one may be open to blame. Anyone who does not provide for their relatives, and especially for their own household, has denied the faith and is worse than an unbeliever.
—1 Timothy 5: 1-8

1. What instructions do these verses give to the sandwich generation?

2. According to these verses, how should members of the same family treat each other?

Near the cross of Jesus stood his mother, his mother's sister, Mary the wife of Clopas, and Mary Magdalene. When Jesus saw his mother there, and the disciple whom he loved standing nearby, he said to her, "Woman, here is your son," and to the disciple, "Here is your mother." From that time on, this disciple took her into his home.
—John 19: 25-27

3. In these verses, Jesus instructs his disciple John to take care of his mother. In what ways do followers of Jesus have care giving respon-

sibility to other members of God's family? Discuss your responses with your group.

"A new command I give you: Love one another. As I have loved you, so you must love one another. By this everyone will know that you are my disciples, if you love one another."
—*John 13:34-35*

Let us not become weary in doing good, for at the proper time we will reap a harvest if we do not give up. Therefore, as we have opportunity, let us do good to all people, especially to those who belong to the family of believers.
—*Galatians 6:9-10*

4. How do the words of Jesus in the first verses relate to the following two verses from Galatians? What is the role of love in care giving?

5. What is the relevance of these verses to the sandwich generation?

YOUR APPLICATION

During the coming week think about and act on the following questions.

1. Are you or anyone you know a member of the sandwich generation? How are you/they handling their situation? If it is you, how can others help you? If it is a friend, how might you help them?

2. Think about and write down specific ways your church or community of Christ followers can help others who are in the sandwich generation, caregiving situations. What can you do to ease the load of family and friends in the sandwich generation?

SESSION 4 | ADULT CHILDREN

INTRODUCTION
Have one or more group members read the introduction aloud.

The Issue: If you have adult children, how can you improve your current relationship with them?

Today, coming of age for young adults is not what it used to be. Many adults in their 20s and 30s are having difficulty launching into adulthood. This struggle was comically depicted in the 2006 movie *Failure to Launch*. The storyline is about a man in his 30s who, like Peter Pan, never grows up. He has no idea how to commit to a mature relationship and feels fine living with his parents. His troubled parents plot to put him in situations that will grow him up and make him independent. Unfortunately, for many young people and aging parents, the failure of young adults to launch is not a laughing matter.

It used to be that once children graduated from high school or college, they would strike out on their own. But times have changed. Dubbed the Boomerang Generation, many young adults stay or return home to live with their parents. There are numerous reasons for this trend. A tough economy and a tight job market coupled with heavy school debt have made it difficult for young adults to become independent. In addition, some experts argue that indulgent parents have created a generation of self-centered trophy kids who believe they are entitled to parental help. While such criticism may be overstated, the return of adult children to their parents' home can create physical, emotional, financial, and spiritual stress.

Even in the majority of aging families where boomerang kids are not present, relationships between parents and their adult children can be tense and stressful. While aging parents and their adult children may love one another, it is still common for feelings of irritation, tension, and ambivalence to exist. Studies have shown that parents usually report more intense tensions than their grown children. Aging parents may have more investment in the relationships and report more tension in their relationships with daughters than with sons. In addition, both sons and daughters report a more strained relationship with their mothers than fathers.

Relational problems between aging parents and their adult children can be caused by a number of common interactions. Most adult children do not appreciate unsolicited parental advice, especially when it is critical of their lifestyle. Tension may result when adult children take advantage of parents as grandkid babysitters. Financial assistance, either from parent to child or child to parent, can create resentment. The aging parent-adult child relationship has a long history and is like no other relationship. While we choose (and unchoose) our friends, the parent-child relationship is given to us for a lifetime.

When it comes to the application of the gospel to parent-adult child relationships, love must be central. Followers of Jesus Christ cannot allow tension and disagreement to fracture these relationships. Jesus clearly calls us to love one another, especially those who are members of our family. As usual, Christian families have an opportunity to model God's ways to a society that has lost its way.

YOUR TAKE

From the following list, check the responses that best answers the questions. Discuss your responses with your group.

1. Which of the following statements best describe your attitude toward your adult child(ren)?

___ I will do whatever I can to help my adult child(ren).

___ I believe my adult child(ren) should learn to make it on their own.

___ I have established specific boundaries and limits with my adult child(ren).

___ I want my adult child(ren) to be completely independent of me.

___ I moved away from my adult child(ren) because they irritate me.

___ I have a wonderful, harmonious relationship with my adult child(ren).

___ I have as little interaction as possible with my adult child(ren).

___ I love my grandkids, but can do without their parents.

___ Other _____.

2. Which of the following areas create the greatest tension between you and your adult child(ren)?

___ Their/your lifestyle   ___ Parenting philosophy

___ Alcohol/drug abuse   ___ Money

___ Values/morality   ___ Politics

___ Spiritual beliefs   ___ Unforgiveness

___ Favoritism   ___ Lack of boundaries

___ Lack of privacy   ___ Lack of respect

___ Media/entertainment choices   ___ Other _____

YOUR REFLECTION

Read the following passages from the Bible and answer the questions that follow.

On the third day a wedding took place at Cana in Galilee. Jesus' mother was there, and Jesus and his disciples had also been invited to the wedding. When the wine was gone, Jesus' mother said to him, "They have no more wine."

"Woman, why do you involve me?" Jesus replied. "My hour has not yet come."

His mother said to the servants, "Do whatever he tells you."
Nearby stood six stone water jars, the kind used by the Jews for ceremonial washing, each holding from twenty to thirty gallons.

Jesus said to the servants, "Fill the jars with water"; so they filled them to the brim.

Then he told them, "Now draw some out and take it to the master of the banquet."

They did so, and the master of the banquet tasted the water that had been turned into wine. He did not realize where it had come from, though the servants who had drawn the water knew. Then he called the bridegroom aside and said, "Everyone brings out the choice wine first and then the cheaper wine after the guests have had too much to drink; but you have saved the best till now."
—John 2: 1-10

1. Why do you think Jesus' mother told him that the wedding host was out of wine?

2. How would you describe Jesus' response to his mother? Was he being disrespectful? If so, why? If not, why not?

3. Why did Jesus turn the water into high quality wine instead of cheap wine?

Then the mother of Zebedee's sons came to Jesus with her sons and, kneeling down, asked a favor of him.

"What is it you want?" he asked.

She said, "Grant that one of these two sons of mine may sit at your right and the other at your left in your kingdom."

"You don't know what you are asking," Jesus said to them. "Can you drink the cup I am going to drink?"

"We can," they answered.

Jesus said to them, "You will indeed drink from my cup, but to sit at my right or left is not for me to grant. These places belong to those for whom they have been prepared by my Father."

When the ten heard about this, they were indignant with the two brothers. Jesus called them together and said, "You know that the rulers of the Gentiles lord it over them, and their high officials exercise authority over them. Not so with you. Instead, whoever wants to become great among you must be your servant, and whoever wants to be first must be your slave—just as the Son of Man did not come to be served, but to serve, and to give his life as a ransom for many."
—Matthew 20:20-28

4. How do you feel about the mother of the sons of Zebedee (James and John) making a special request of Jesus? Is James' and John's mother different or similar to contemporary mothers? Please explain your response.

5. Why were the other disciples upset about the mother's request?

6. How is Jesus' response to the request relevant to us today?

YOUR APPLICATION

During the coming week think about and act on the following questions.

1. If you have adult children, how would you assess your current relationship? How did this/these relationship(s) get to its/their current state?

2. What practical steps can you take to improve your relationship(s) with your adult child(ren)? Write down these steps and begin to act on them. (Start this whole process with prayer.)

SESSION 5 | EMPTY NEST

INTRODUCTION
Have one or more group members read the introduction aloud.

The Issue: As children leave home, a transition into a new stage of life takes place. How have you managed or will you manage the empty nest stage of your life?

The empty nest stage is another transition experienced by many older adults. Many parents experience mixed emotions when the last child leaves home. There may be elation and joy in response to a new found freedom. Or there may be sadness and loss as this new stage of life takes hold.

While women can be more affected by an empty nest, men are not immune from the feelings of loss as the last child departs. In some cases, empty nest feelings go beyond sadness to depression or grief as parents find it difficult to have no children at home. Empty nest parents may also find themselves worrying intensely about the safety of their child or children and whether they will be able to take care of themselves. In general, the parents that have the greatest difficulty with the empty nest transition are those who cannot or will not let their children move into independent adulthood. When empty nest parents see their children struggle and come to the rescue, they usually do a disservice to themselves and their children.

On the flip side, the empty nest stage can be a wonderful time of freedom and reinvention. Empty nest parents have a new opportunity to reconnect with each other. They can work on the improvement of their marriage and rekindle interests that have lied dormant while they raised children. When couples communicate well and plan ahead, they can make the empty nest stage enjoyable and full of new beginnings.

Still, the empty nest stage can bring numerous changes that place new stresses on the best of marriages. It is wise for a couple to be proactive in discussing and talking about how they will handle these changes together. The following are just a few of the changes and issues that can be addressed by empty nest couples:

- What are your hopes and dreams for the future?
- Will we handle our finances differently now?
- Will we be spending too much/not enough time together now?
- How will we handle boomerang kids who want to move back home?
- Will our roles in the family change?
- Should we downsize our lifestyle?
- What are our expectations for the empty nest stage?
- Should we travel more? If so, where and why?

These and many other changes and possibilities need to be discussed and thought through to make the empty nest years a time of thriving and not merely surviving.

For followers of Jesus Christ, the empty nest stage can be particularly exciting. Many parents have put God's call on their lives on the back burner as they spend their time and energy raising kids. The empty nest stage can allow parents to hit the reset button and revisit God's fresh call on their lives. With many years of life experience under their belt, empty nesters are a valuable resource for God's kingdom. For many, it is now less risky to take that leap of faith that will move them toward their sweet spot in God's kingdom. Together with a group of friends, begin to explore creative ways you can minister effectively during the empty nest stage.

YOUR TAKE

From the following list, check the responses that best answers the questions. Discuss your responses with your group.

1. What happened or what do you think will happen when your child/children left or will leave home?

___ You leave their bedroom untouched.

___ Your phone rings less.

__ You get more text messages.

__ Your house stays clean.

__ There is food in the refrigerator.

__ The water bill takes a dive.

__ Your house becomes your kid's storage area.

__ Your home is quiet.

__ You wash clothes less.

__ You cut the grass.

__ You still stay up worrying about your kids.

__ Your home is boring.

__ You have to take care of the dog.

__ Your grocery bill decreases.

__ You pray a lot more for your children.

__ Other _____.

2. Which of the following statements best expresses your feelings about the empty nest stage of life?

__ I am saddened by the thought of my child or children leaving home.

__ I couldn't or can't wait until the kid or kids are out of the house.

__ I think the empty nest stage is exciting.

__ I want to try some things I have put off.

__ My relationship with God has grown or will grow during this time.

__ I am or will be totally disoriented during the empty nest stage.

__ I am or will be more open to change during this stage.

__ I need to work hard not to interfere in the life of my child or children.

__ I feel or will feel useless without children at home.

__ Other _____.

YOUR REFLECTION

Read the following passages from the Bible and answer the questions that follow.

Jesus continued: "There was a man who had two sons. The younger one said to his father, 'Father, give me my share of the estate.' So he divided his property between them.

"Not long after that, the younger son got together all he had, set off for a distant country and there squandered his wealth in wild living. After he had spent everything, there was a severe famine in that whole country, and he began to be in need. So he went and hired himself out to a citizen of that country, who sent him to his fields to feed pigs. He longed to fill his stomach with the pods that the pigs were eating, but no one gave him anything.

"When he came to his senses, he said, 'How many of my father's hired servants have food to spare, and here I am starving to death! I will set out and go back to my father and say to him: Father, I have sinned against heaven and against you. I am no longer worthy to be called your son; make me like one of your hired servants.' So he got up and went to his father.

"But while he was still a long way off, his father saw him and was filled with compassion for him; he ran to his son, threw his arms around him and kissed him.

"The son said to him, 'Father, I have sinned against heaven and against you. I am no longer worthy to be called your son.'

"But the father said to his servants, 'Quick! Bring the best robe and put it on him. Put a ring on his finger and sandals on his feet. Bring the fattened calf and kill it. Let's have a feast and celebrate. For this son of mine was dead and is alive again; he was lost and is found.' So they began to celebrate.

"Meanwhile, the older son was in the field. When he came near the house, he heard music and dancing. So he called one of the servants

and asked him what was going on. 'Your brother has come,' he replied, 'and your father has killed the fattened calf because he has him back safe and sound.'

"The older brother became angry and refused to go in. So his father went out and pleaded with him. But he answered his father, 'Look! All these years I've been slaving for you and never disobeyed your orders. Yet you never gave me even a young goat so I could celebrate with my friends. But when this son of yours who has squandered your property with prostitutes comes home, you kill the fattened calf for him!'

"'My son,' the father said, 'you are always with me, and everything I have is yours. But we had to celebrate and be glad, because this brother of yours was dead and is alive again; he was lost and is found.'"
—Luke 15:11-32

1. Why do you think Jesus told this parable to the Pharisees?

2. Why didn't the father object to the younger son's request for his inheritance? What would you have done?

3. When children leave home, what are some of the feelings empty nest parents can have?

4. When the younger son returned, why didn't the father scold and punish him for his foolish behavior?

5. In what ways can the empty nest stage amplify sibling rivalry? Was the father fair to both his sons?

6. Do you believe that empty nest parents need to allow their children to learn through experience? Please explain your response.

7. Why and how is this parable a universal story about mankind?

YOUR APPLICATION

During the coming week think about and act on the following exercises and questions.

1. Take some time this week to think about the empty nest stage in your life. If you are in this stage, how can you make it better? If the empty nest stage is in your future, what steps can you take to make it a smoother transition?

2. Schedule some time this week to think and pray about the empty nest stage in your life. Specifically, write down your hopes and expectations for this time of life. Most importantly, think and pray about how God wants you to use this special time. Write down and act on the answers and clarity that comes.

SESSION 6 | THE AGING MARRIAGE

INTRODUCTION
Have one or more group members read the introduction aloud.

The Issue: How are you responding to the changes that come in the second half of marriage?

Most couples enter marriage with the plan to live happily ever after. Unfortunately, many marriages end before "death do us part." The United States has the highest divorce rate in the world and older marriages are not immune from the statistics. The divorce rate for older adults has doubled since 1980 with 1 in 4 divorces involving people over 50 years of age. This is not what God intended for marriage.

Marriages in the second half of life are not on automatic pilot...they still need work and attention. Couples in long lasting marriages know that there is no such thing as a perfect marriage. Every marriage has its ups and downs, but successful couples stay committed and don't bail out. Instead of looking for exit strategies, couples in long lasting marriages seek solutions when they hit rough spots.

Researchers have recorded the advice of couples who have been married for many years. Here are some of the tips they offer to younger couples:

- Continue to build intimacy, both sexually and emotionally, throughout your marriage.
- Forgive one another and don't hold on to past hurts.
- Comfort, encourage, and affirm one another.
- Create passion for life and one another.
- Control your anger and avoid abuse.
- Accept your differences and don't try to change one another.
- Spend some time together every day.
- Say "I love you" to each other regularly.
- Affirm and celebrate your commitment to one another regularly.
- Be friends as well as lovers.

- Have fun together and laugh together.
- Be open to compromising and negotiating.
- Parent together.
- Respect one another's need for privacy and space.
- Encourage each other in your spiritual journeys.

There are many other ways an aging couple can keep their marriage vital, interesting, and alive.

For Christian couples, the second half of marriage can be an exciting time when their love grows deeper. With the children out of the house, careers winding down, less financial pressures, and other changes, couples can take the time to reaffirm their love and get to know each other in new and more meaningful ways. During this time there are many opportunities to creatively minister together, but couples must proactively pursue them. Today, more than ever in our lifetime, followers of Jesus Christ need to show the way on how to have a long lasting, successful marriage that is glorifying to God.

YOUR TAKE

From the following lists, check the responses that best answers the questions. Discuss your responses with your group.

1. Which of the following are the greatest challenges and issues for couples in the second half of marriage?

___ Dealing with health issues

___ Relating to adult children

___ Keeping your job

___ Making decisions on travel

___ Taking care of grandchildren

___ Trying to grow spiritually

___ Finding life boring

___ Taking care of aging parents

___ Having difficulty communicating

___ Having too much time alone

___ Not having enough fun

___ Keeping marriage interesting

___ Meeting financial pressures

___ Making retirement decisions

___ Deciding on downsizing

__ Keeping up your house

__ Getting along as a couple

__ Finding an interesting hobby

__ Having too little time

__ Not having enough time alone

__ Learning to fight fair

__ Other _____

2. Which of the following would you give as advice to a young married couple?

__ Stay committed

__ Have fun together

__ Fight fair

__ Get on the same parenting page

__ Keep romance alive

__ Learn some independence

__ Listen well

__ Do things together

__ Celebrate birthdays, holidays, etc.

__ Develop your spiritual lives together

__ Compliment your spouse

__ Deal with crisis together

__ Talk about your emotions

__ Get along with in-laws

__ Study the Bible together

__ Appreciate your differences

__ Work to change each other

__ Forgive each other often

__ Compromise and negotiate

__ Respect one another

__ Give each other space when necessary

__ Don't criticize your spouse

__ Plan regular date nights

__ Be kind to each other

__ Pray together

__ Say "I love you" often

__ Stay physically fit

__ Have a good sense of humor

__ Do work you love

__ Other _____

YOUR REFLECTION

Read the following passages from the Bible and answer the questions that follow.

Wives, submit yourselves to your own husbands as you do to the Lord. For the husband is the head of the wife as Christ is the head of the church, his body, of which he is the Savior. Now as the church submits to Christ, so also wives should submit to their husbands in everything.

Husbands, love your wives, just as Christ loved the church and gave himself up for her to make her holy, cleansing her by the washing with water through the word, and to present her to himself as a radiant church, without stain or wrinkle or any other blemish, but holy and blameless. In this same way, husbands ought to love their wives as their own bodies. He who loves his wife loves himself. After all, no one ever hated their own body, but they feed and care for their body, just as Christ does the church—for we are members of his body. "For this reason a man will leave his father and mother and be united to his wife, and the two will become one flesh." This is a profound mystery— but I am talking about Christ and the church. However, each one of you also must love his wife as he loves himself, and the wife must respect her husband.
—Ephesians 5:22-28

1. Why have these verses become controversial today? How well does each of us generally handle submission?

2. Do you see these verses as descriptive or prescriptive? That is, do they describe marriages in Jesus' day or are they giving us guidelines on how marriages work today?

3. In what practical ways is love central to a healthy, long lasting marriage?

Wives, in the same way submit yourselves to your own husbands so that, if any of them do not believe the word, they may be won over without words by the behavior of their wives, when they see the purity and reverence of your lives. Your beauty should not come from outward adornment, such as elaborate hairstyles and the wearing of gold jewelry or fine clothes. Rather, it should be that of your inner self, the unfading beauty of a gentle and quiet spirit, which is of great worth in God's sight. For this is the way the holy women of the past who put their hope in God used to adorn themselves. They submitted themselves to their own husbands, like Sarah, who obeyed Abraham and called him her lord. You are her daughters if you do what is right and do not give way to fear.

Husbands, in the same way be considerate as you live with your wives, and treat them with respect as the weaker partner and as heirs with you of the gracious gift of life, so that nothing will hinder your prayers.
—1 Peter 3:1-7

4. Do these verses imply that the woman should be the spiritual leader in a marriage? How can couples in the second half of marriage encourage each other in spiritual growth?

5. How would you contrast outer and inner beauty? What relevance does beauty have to a long, lasting marriage?

6. Numerous verses in the Bible instruct men to love their wives. In what ways is a husband's love central to a healthy, long lasting marriage?

YOUR APPLICATION

During the coming week think about and act on the following exercises and questions.

1. On a scale of 1 to 10, with 1 being very unhealthy and 10 being very healthy, what is currently the health of your marriage?

1	2	3	4	5	6	7	8	9	10

2. If your marriage is not a 10, what can you do to move it closer to a 10? The following are some suggestions that might help.

___ Spend more time communicating as a couple.

___ Spend more time having fun together.

___ Concentrate less on work and more on your relationship.

___ Plan regular date nights.

___ Create passion for life and one another.

___ Communicate and celebrate your commitment to one another.

___ Comfort, encourage, and affirm one another.

___ Don't try to change one another.

FURTHER READING

The Family: A Christian Perspective on the Contemporary Home by Jack O. Balswick and Judith K. Balswick

Unwrapping the Sandwich Generation. Life Vignettes about Seniors & Their Adult Boomer Children by Susan Cunningham

Walking on Eggshells: Navigating the Delicate Relationship Between Adult Children and Parents by Jane Isay

The Marriage You've Always Wanted by Gary Chapman

Thriving in the Empty Nest—Word Document [Download] by *Christianity Today International*

The Second Half of Marriage by David and Claudia Arp

ABOUT THE AUTHOR

Peter Menconi has written and presented widely on generational and aging issues. His rich background as a dentist, pastor, counselor, business owner, conference speaker, husband, father, and grandfather brings unique perspectives to his writing.

Born and raised in Chicago, Pete graduated from the University of Illinois, College of Dentistry and practiced dentistry for 23 years in private practice, in the U.S. Army and in a mission hospital in Kenya, East Africa. In addition, Pete has a M.S. in Counseling Psychology and several years of seminary training. He has also been a commodity futures floor trader, a speaker with the American Dental Association, and a broker of medical and dental practices.

For over 20 years Pete was the outreach pastor at a large church in suburban Denver, Colorado. Currently, he is the president of Mt. Sage Publishing and board member with the CASA Network.

Pete's writings include the book *The Intergenerational Church: Understanding Congregations from WWII to www.com*, The Support Group Series, a 9-book Bible study series, and numerous articles.

Pete and his wife Jean live in the Denver area and they are the parents of 3 adult children and the grandparents of 9 grandchildren.

Pete Menconi can be reached at petermenconi@msn.com.

CASA NETWORK

AGING WELL

BIBLE STUDY SERIES

Finally, a Bible study series for everyone 50 and over who wants to stay in the game as long as possible!

THE AGING CHALLENGE

The primary purpose of this Bible study is to help you take a fresh look at aging, reevaluate your current situation, and consider making some changes.

THE NEW R & R: RETIRED AND REWIRED

The primary purpose of this Bible study is to help you to take a fresh look at retirement, reevaluate your current situation, and consider making some changes.

GENERATIONS TOGETHER

The primary purpose of this Bible study is to help you to take a fresh look at our current generations, how the generations relate, and how we can be better together.

SAGE OR CURMUDGEON

The primary purpose of this Bible study is to help you to take a closer look at your attitude about aging, how to reevaluate your attitude, and how to move toward becoming a sage for younger people.

THE AGING FAMILY AND MARRIAGE

The primary purpose of this Bible study is to help you to take a closer look at your aging marriage and/or family and see how you can maximize these relationships.

FINISHING WELL

The primary purpose of this Bible study is to help you to take a closer look at how you can finish well before your life is over.

THE INTERGENERATIONAL CHURCH:
Understanding Congregations from
WWII to www.com

Are certain generations underrepresented in your church?

Would you like to see more young adults in your congregation?

The Intergenerational Church: Understanding Congregations from WWII to www.com will show you why understanding today's generations is crucial for the survival and thrival of the local church.

The Intergenerational Church is a breakthrough book that will help you meet the Intergenerational Challenge.

FROM THIS IMPORTANT BOOK, YOU WILL LEARN HOW TO:

- Minimize generational tension.
- Get all the generations moving in the same direction.
- Develop leaders from all generations.
- Deliver intergenerational preaching.
- Cultivate intergenerational worship and community.
- Stimulate intergenerational mission and outreach.

Made in the USA
San Bernardino, CA
06 November 2013